Unicorn Time

**Poems and Illustrations
by Aaron Brossoit**

Trade ISBN: 978-0-615-92493-9

Dedicated in loving memory
to my cat
Guinness

Table of Contents

Unicorn Time

There are funny spans of time
you can't anticipate.
Like from a nursery rhyme
they seem to apparate.

A meeting is pushed back,
or your guest is running late.
Your plans fly off the track
and you have to sit and wait.

That's a very special time
that magically appears.
You have no obligations
to any of your peers.

Like a sparkly unicorn
You find time to rest your feet.
Magically relaxing,
a personal retreat.

It's the perfect time for music
or to write a thank you note.
It's in this very special time
the greatest poems were "wrote".

No one's going to ever know.
The time's a mystery.
Like the unicorns of stories
it was never meant to be.

Grizzly Bear

I wish I had a grizzly bear.
My friends would think it's cool.
Behind its neck, I'd grab its hair
and ride the bear to school.

All the kids that ever teased me
would know it ate whatever pleased me!
Plus they'd see me live on TV
with a grizzly bear beneath me.

If I had a grizzly bear.

"What Was That?"

"What was that?"
I lost you there.
Before you said that other thing.
That's when I quit remembering
and started reassembling.

Somewhere in our current chat,
I lost the place where I was at
and now I can't remember why
I just asked you, "What was that?"

Dinosaur Sounds

Diplodicus, Shmiplodicus!
I'm not afraid of dinosaurs.
Sure they left gigantic bones
but who's to say they had loud roars?

Tyrannosaurus, Bananasaurus!
They may have gnashed their sharpened teeth
but sounded just like little cats
or teeny, weeny birdy tweets.

Unfortunately,
we'll never know.
Dinosaurs
died long ago.

Wings

Do you think a snake
begs for legs?
Or a bird
wishes for things?

Cause I'm a guy
who would love to fly
and begs and wishes
for wings.

I Planned For That

I came across a slippery slope.
I planned for that,
I brought some rope.

The desert sand got even hotter.
I planned for that,
I brought some water.

The cold and dark, it made me tire,
but I brought a flint
to start a fire.

And when my eyes began to sag,
I'm glad I packed
a sleeping bag.

No matter what might come my way
I planned for it a previous day.

And if I find I'm not prepared,
I'll plan on being really scared!

Trust

Give somebody all your trust
and they could do you wrong.
Make somebody earn your trust
and it will take too long.

If you make a test for trust
then trust was never here.
If you choose to never trust
you'll live your life in fear.

So what's the right amount of trust
to give to someone new?
Just trust your gut and give the trust
you hope they'll give to you.

Meditate

I'm trying hard to meditate
breathing long and slow,
to let my mind recuperate
and let my thoughts all go.

I'm trying hard to meditate
here quiet in my home.
But my brain within its current state
is thinking through this poem.

Kite

I really love to fly this kite.
There's something that just feels right.
The wind it pulls the string so tight
and flies it to a greater height.

And now the kite is out of sight,
but something doesn't seem quite right.
I wish there was a bit more light.
It's hard to fly this kite at night.

Redwood Tree

The
redwood
is
my favorite
tree,
the tallest
tree
that is to be.
I feel
like a little pea.
They're
30 stories tall!
It
occurred to me
the
redwood tree
saw
most of human
history,
but now it's time
for
me to be the
one
who
loves
it all.

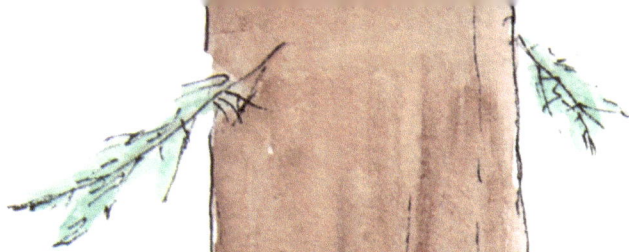

The Path

I followed the path
over the hill
past the stream
through the woods
under the bridge
into the mud
near the cave

and that is where
I saw the bear
In the cave just sitting there.
I did not dare
to stop and stare,
no time to spare
with such a scare!

I ran from the cave
back into the mud
back under the bridge
back through the woods
back past the stream
back over the hill
and followed this path, you see,

to share this scare
about the bear
close on the path behind me!

Going Bananas

I'm going bananas!
I can't figure out
what the big deal
is all about.

Is it 'cause they are yellow?
Or shaped like a smile?
'Cause monkeys devour them
up by the pile?

And why is it funny
when they fall on the ground?
I don't want bananas
just lying around.

I don't like the feel
of hitting the floor
when I slip on a peel
a banana once wore.

I'll turn that smile
into a frown!
I'll just flip your banana
upside down!

I'm going bananas!
And nobody cares.
I just know nobody
ever goes "PEARS!"

Certain Future

There is one thing that is certain.
One thing that's always true.
No matter what your plans are
or what you hope to do.

One certain thing to count on
no matter what the deed.
And while the final plans are made,
indeed this thing is guaranteed.

It's repeated throughout history
yet leaves our geniuses perplexed.
It still remains a mystery
exactly what will happen next.

Fairytale Hygiene

If you ever kiss a slimy frog
it may turn into a prince,
either way I'd recommend
to give your lips a thorough rinse!

Today

Grab a glass and raise it high!
I'd like to dedicate this toast
to a very special time...

Today.

The day I love the most.

More than days of time gone by,
yesterday and days no more.
Today's the day I love the most
because there's still time left in store!

Where Did All the Monsters Go?

Where did all the monsters go?
The scary ones with all the hair.
Where did all the monsters go?
The closet's dark, but nothing's there!

No more tentacles or teeth
No more growly, gnarly noise
No more nasty monster breath
to frighten sleeping girls and boys.

I just cannot figure out
where the monsters might have gone,
I thought that they were all about
before I flipped the light switch on.

Wizard

I think my dad's a wizard.
He's been acting kind of weird.
He always wears this funny hat
and has a long white beard.

He's in the kitchen every day
conjuring up spells.
I just hope that dinner tastes
better than it smells!

Experts

The experts in the world,
they want to share with you.
No matter what you're planning
they know just what to do

If you have some good ideas,
you'll see that they have more,
'cause they got their expertise
when they made mistakes before.

They solved a problem from the past
from a certain point of view,
but times and circumstances change.
Solutions need to, too!

So instead, just do your own thing,
original and new.
Make your own mistakes
and become an expert too!

A is for Apple

Alex ate an apple.
Bobby bit before.
Cathy can't quit coughing 'cause she tried to eat the core.
Donald did a double dare
Eating every seed,
Finally falling flat from feeling funny from his deed.

Cowboy Courting

Cowboy Bob loved cattle
grazing on the plain.
When Bob came in from ranching,
he courted cowgirl Jane.

Cowboy Bob loved cattle.
Cowgirl Jane did too.
But when Bob brought one on a date
Jane said, "BOB, WE'RE THROUGH!"

The Fastest Man

The fastest man in all the land
ran all alone across the sand.
His services were in demand
to bring things places fast.

The fastest man would not retreat
from desert heat upon his feet.
The sandy storms that he did meet
would only blow on past.

So you then must understand,
the fastest man in all the land
would never get a helping hand
so that his fame would last.

But I'm afraid this latest feat
the fastest man will not repeat.
Defeat did meet his broken feet
and now he has a cast!

Cause Today

I am going to cause today
to happen in a different way.
To say the things I've meant to say
or talk to someone new.

To cause a project to be made
or cause some music to be played
or cause a hammock in the shade!
Because I caused it to.

Today I'm going to cause to be
different from all history!
It's destiny. And time for me
to go and make it true.

THΩN

THΩN is a mighty redwood god
you've never seen before.
He watches over redwood trees
and guards the forest floor.

He's stump born of the oldest tree
with spider plants for hair.
Through THΩN's glowing seashell eyes
on every soul he'll stare.

Animals from every way
don't hesitate to kneel and pray.
Treasures at his base they lay
to hear THΩN say, "I bless your day."

THΩN's a mighty redwood god
so isn't it a shame,
that no one can agree on
how to pronounce his name.

Hey You!

Hey You! Don't stare at me.
I'll be how I want to be.
To be the personality
that I would be live on TV!

Hey You! Look inside
through the back of those eyes you've opened wide.
You've been floating with the tide.
Come with me! Let's take a ride!

Hey You! Now you see
It's you and me in symphony.
With a little creativity
we can seize an opportunity.

That's the way
it's supposed to be.
You and me
in symphony.

Forest Woman

There's a woman with a guitar
who lives in the forest,
a beautiful woman
who sings forest songs.

Her music is magic,
old songs of the forest,
the stories are tragic
yet the old she still longs.

When nature everywhere
was ruled by wolf and bear,
the shark in sea and hawk in air.
Simple rights and wrongs.

She sings on high
of times gone by.
Brings a tear to a woodsmen's eye.
Each chord reminding him that he belongs.

Ukulele

Ukulele 'lele 'lele.
Playing lots of ukulele.
Lately ukulele is
the coolest thing to play!

Ukulele 'lele 'lele
It's fun to play the ukulele
Ukelele, ukelele, ukelele 'le!

Ukulele 'lele 'lele.
Sing along with ukulele.
Playing all the ukulele
songs we want all day!

Ukulele 'lele 'lele.
Two can play the ukulele.
Ukelele, ukelele, ukelele 'le!

Ukulele lady likes my
ukulele 'lele likes to
dance the hula, hula
when my ukulele plays!

Ukulele 'lele 'lele.
Dancing to the ukulele.
Ukelele, ukelele, ukelele 'le!

Ukulele 'lele 'lele.
Playing lots of ukulele.
Lately ukulele is
the coolest thing to play!

Perspective

Your glass can be half empty
or it can be half full.
Points of view will differ based on
what's inside the bowl.

82 Things to Do

1. Take a walk
2. Ride your bike
3. Draw with chalk
4. Take a hike
5. Spot a bird
6. Hum a tune
7. Invent a word
8. Eat at noon
9. Find a lake
10. Climb a tree
11. Bake a cake
12. Bring cake to me!
13. Rollerskate
14. Toss a ball
15. Meditate
16. Paint a wall
17. Find a bone
18. Take a shower
19. Find the phone
20. It's out of power
21. Set up camp
22. Play a game
23. Build a ramp
24. Dream of fame
25. Downhill ski
26. Drink some tea
27. Plant a tree
28. Write to me
29. Build a fort
30. Sail a boat
31. Play a sport
32. Rootbeer float!
33. Grow a plant
34. Grow some food
35. Go and rant
36. Have attitude!
37. Wear a hat
38. Wear a smile
39. Pet a cat
40. Run a mile
41. See a sunrise
42. and sunset
43. Close your eyes
44. Don't forget!
45. Swim a lap
46. Write a poem
47. Take a nap
48. Clean the home
49. Be a cook
50. Shave your head
51. Get two books
52. you haven't read
53. Fly a kite
54. Smell a flower
55. Start a fight
56. Climb a tower
57. Bury a chest
58. Make a map
59. Take a test
60. Write a rap
61. Draw a sketch
62. Climb a rope
63. Go play catch
64. Smell some soap
65. Make a path
66. Train a dog
67. Do some math
68. Lift a log
69. Call your mommy
70. Daddy, too
71. Do origami
72. Dress in blue
73. Carve a stick
74. Tie your shoe
75. Learn a trick
76. Find a clue
77. Stand up proud!
78. Raise a fist
79. Yell really loud!
80. Add what I missed
81. Still you're bored?
82. Re-read this list.

Wooden Ship

I was sailing in a wooden ship
moving at a steady clip.
I never meant to take a dip
but dropped my knife and caused a chip.
At first the chip just sprang a drip,
a little drip that I could sip
and hold securely with my lip.
But then the boards began to rip.
Bracing hard so not to slip,
I tried to hold it with my hip
but water hit me like a whip.
I think I did a double flip!
That's when the boat began to tip

I never meant to take a dip!

Procrastination

There is something I'm supposed to do
I ought to do today.
In fact it was the thing to do
when it was yesterday.

But now that I have found the time
to get that something done…
Instead I wrote another rhyme
and had a lot more fun!

Photo Credits: Angel

About the Author

Aaron Brossoit created these poems and illustrations from the Santa Cruz Mountains with endless inspiration from the redwood trees, banana slugs, ukuleles and all the crazy people living out there (including himself.)

A note from the author:
Special thanks to my wonderful wife Angel, my editor Mom, and all my nieces and nephews for continued motivation and support.

www.ingramcontent.com/pod-product-compliance
Lightning Source LLC
LaVergne TN
LVHW010029070426
835511LV00004B/97